To my new friend and
Rec. Instructor T.
 It is my prayer
that as you read and
study this book you
will find truth and
peace, and that God
will continue to bless
you as you serve Him

 Your brother in Christ
 John

What Makes a
Christian a
Disciple of Christ?

JOHN S. JOHNSON

WESTBOW
PRESS®
A DIVISION OF THOMAS NELSON
& ZONDERVAN

THE HOLY BIBLE, NEW INTERNATIONAL VERSION®, NIV® Copyright © 1973, 1978, 1984, 2011 by Biblica, Inc.® Used by permission. All rights reserved worldwide.

All Greek Definitions are from the The Strongest NIV Exhaustive Concordance, Edward W. Goodrick and John R Kohlenberger III, 1990

All English Definitions are from the Merriam Webster's Collegiate Dictionary, Tenth Edition, Principal Copyright 1993

Artist name: Sandra Johnson

This book is a work of non-fiction. Unless otherwise noted, the author and the publisher make no explicit guarantees as to the accuracy of the information contained in this book and in some cases, names of people and places have been altered to protect their privacy.

WestBow Press books may be ordered through booksellers or by contacting:

WestBow Press
A Division of Thomas Nelson & Zondervan
1663 Liberty Drive
Bloomington, IN 47403
www.westbowpress.com
1 (866) 928-1240

ISBN: 978-1-5127-4782-9 (sc)
ISBN: 978-1-5127-4783-6 (hc)
ISBN: 978-1-5127-4784-3 (e)

Library of Congress Control Number: 2016910525

Print information available on the last page.

WestBow Press rev. date: 07/20/2016

Contents

Note from John

I want to share some of the reasons I decided to compile this study book.

I first believed in the Gospel of Jesus Christ when I was twenty-seven years old, and as of this writing I have been a believer for fifty years. I am a seasoned citizen and have been around the block a few times. In the early years as I was developing my own walk with Jesus, I think it was based mainly on my love for Him and for what He did for me.

We know that love for Jesus must be our first and last love. It was like being on cloud nine, but eventually we must come down out of the clouds. As we return to earth we begin to experience turbulence and then it is back to reality.

The question began to come – what is my real purpose as a Christian? Since Jesus has all power and authority in heaven and earth, why did He leave the earth and expect Christians to continue His work and message? How can I make a difference?

There were many other questions and prayers to God. He said to me, "Through My word, if you are willing, I will show you examples of your questions and prayers through your own life." This happened about nine years after I first believed, Like Isaiah, I said, "here am I, send me".

God sent my wife, three daughters and me to two different countries. We were one year in Switzerland and three years in Cote d'Ivoire, West Africa. You might say, "he is a missionary so he knows the Bible inside and out." Here is the point – you can know the Bible inside and out and not really understand much of it.

As the years keep clicking off I must admit I still don't know much and I am still learning. I don't know how many times I wished I would have known this earlier in my Christian life.

I have compiled this study book with basic truths, so that if we can understand and grasp them, it will make our walk with Jesus sweeter each day.

As we each read this book, may we gain insight that will help us live the Spirit-filled life.

Dedication

I dedicate this book first to my immediate family: to my wife, Sandie; children, Stacie and Mike, Terrie and Hal, Sallie and Burt; to my grandchildren, Anna and Scott, John and Rachell, Jason and Lauren, Kiersten and Nathanael, Brock, Dawson, Nathan, Summer, Zachary and Aubree; to my great-grandchildren, Grant, Claire, Logan, Gwen, Alex, Joshua and Jude; and to those who are the future born; also, to all my brothers and sisters in Christ around the world.

Acknowledgements

I wish to extend a special thank you to my family and friends who diligently encouraged, supported me in prayer, and helped in the research, printing and editing of this book to make it possible.

First, to my wife, Sandie and daughters, Stacie, Terrie and Sallie; also to my Men's Bible Study group, Ken, Jim, Mike, Roy, and Justin who took the time to critique this project, and to Betty who kept the coffee and goodies coming.

A Note To The Leader

This study book is for all Christians. Mature believers can be refreshed and new believers can learn basic truths for living a spiritual life. Each chapter has its own theme and the comments and questions are meant to stimulate discussion.

The leader is encouraged to guide the discussion and keep it on point. It is important to start each session by breaking up in two's and reciting memory verses.

Getting Started -

What Makes A Christian A Disciple Of Christ?

Memory Verse: Matthew 28:18–20
> Then Jesus came to them and said, "All authority in heaven and on earth has been given to me. Therefore go and make disciples of all nations, baptizing them in the name of the Father and of the Son and of the Holy Spirit, and teaching them to obey everything I have commanded you. And surely I am with you always, to the very end of the age."

A disciple is one being taught by a teacher. Pretty simple stuff isn't it? Only in this case, our lives depend on it! Jesus said to go make disciples. We need to understand what He meant by *make*. This study will, by no means, exhaust everything it takes to make a disciple. Its purpose is to focus on some of the essential truths that a Christian must know and apply to his life.

Discipleship is a process of commitment to learn to become like Jesus. To find God's will takes a commitment of time in perseverance, faithfulness, memorization of His Word and prayer. This process equips us to teach believers to become disciples, ultimately to become more like Christ. The memory verses, Matthew 28:18–20, are the basis for and of Christian discipleship. This is *The Great Commission.*

First of all Jesus backs up his command by saying, "...all authority in heaven and on earth has been given to me." This is a declaration of his sovereignty. The sovereignty of God and the responsibility of man is an abiding principle throughout the Bible, Old and New Testaments. God's sovereignty is seen in "...all authority in heaven and on earth has been given to me...", and the responsibility of man is seen in "Therefore go and make disciples of all nations, baptizing them in the name of the Father and of the Son and of the Holy Spirit, and teaching them to obey everything I have commanded you." Again, we see God's sovereignty at the end of this passage, "...and surely I am with you always, to the end of the age."

We read Matthew 28:18–20. Now let's read companion verses in Mark 16:15–16, "He said to them, 'Go into all the world and preach the gospel to all creation. Whoever believes and is baptized will be saved, but whoever does not believe will be condemned.'"

We see that the one who is commanded to be taught is the one who believes and is baptized and saved. The teachers Jesus is speaking to are all the apostles and disciples who were gathered there.

Concerning the commands of Jesus, often there is some misunderstanding. There are those who believe that the only commands that are important are in John 13:34-35. Read these verses so that we know what Jesus is saying. What He is saying is He wanted to tell the disciples He is giving a new commandment. He is not saying this is the only commandment. As we know, in the New Testament Jesus stated many commands for his followers. Yes, Jesus commands us to love God, love our brothers and sisters, and love our neighbors; but within the context of that love, there is a sense of obedience to everything else that Jesus commands.

We will be discussing this more in Chapter 2, the chapter about love, but for now, keep in mind that throughout his ministry and teaching his followers, He used words like *seek, do, do not, go, pray,* etc. These are all commands of Jesus.

The desired purpose of this book is to study truths that are basic and essential in teaching believers to become more like Jesus and to live the Spirit-filled life. The Bible is the handbook for life that is God breathed (inspired by God), and is the absolute truth.

For this book we want to have a personal motto concerning God's Word and this is it:

God said it! I believe it! That settles it!

Welcome to the Way, the Truth and the Life!

truly I tell you....", Whenever Jesus says "very truly," He is saying, "Listen up or pay attention!" When He says, "Whoever hears my word...", it appears He is talking about His Word. Then He says, "... and believes him who sent me..." Jesus is talking about the Father who sent Him. Finally, He says, "...has eternal life and will not be judged but has crossed over from death to life." What is Jesus actually saying here? We know that in order to be saved and have eternal life we must put our belief and trust in Jesus. God's plan was to send Jesus. Jesus, the Son, came as planned. The Holy Spirit was involved in his conception and empowered him to do what He did. So we see, right there in a nutshell, God the Father, God the Son and God the Holy Spirit were involved in salvation.

In no way are we necessarily discussing the doctrine of the Trinity in this study. We are pointing out that by believing in One, we believe in all three because the Three are One. We cannot just believe in Jesus without believing in God and his Holy Spirit.

Read Luke 1:28–35. It shows that the Father, Son and Holy Spirit were involved in Jesus' conception.

Now read John 1:29–34. John the Baptist is confirming that Christ is the anointed One. There were signs from God the Father and God the Holy Spirit that this is truly the anointed One.

In reading 2 Corinthians 1:21–22, we see that the work being done in these verses is done by the Father, Son and Holy Spirit.

The three portions of scripture above reveal that the Trinity (God the Father, God the Son, God the Holy Spirit) is involved in God's plan of salvation (the gospel).

Again, we are pointing out that by believing in One, we believe in the Three because the Three are One. We cannot just believe in Jesus without believing in God the Father and His Holy Spirit.

Believing is the trigger of salvation. The only way to come to the Father is explained in John 14:5–6 "Thomas said to him, 'Lord, we don't know where you are going, so how can we know the way?' Jesus answered, 'I am the way and the truth and the life. No one comes to the Father except through me.'"

Believe! The Father draws one to Jesus as one believes God's Word and the work of Jesus.

John 6:44–45

> No one can come to me unless the Father who sent me draws them, and I will raise them up at the last day. It is written in the Prophets: 'They will all be taught by God.' Everyone who has heard the Father and learned from him comes to Me. (see Isaiah 54:13)

Believe!

Romans 10:9–10

> If you declare with your mouth, "Jesus is Lord," and believe in your heart that God raised him from the dead, you will be saved. For it is with your heart that you believe and are justified, and it is with your mouth that you profess your faith and are saved.

We need to keep in mind and understand that there are warnings from the Scriptures about unbelief.

John 3:17–18,

> For God did not send His Son into the world to condemn the world, but to save the world through Him. Whoever believes in him is not condemned, but whoever does not believe stands condemned already because they have not believed in the name of God's one and only Son.

1 Corinthians 15:2 says, "By this gospel you are saved, if you hold firmly to the word I preached to you. Otherwise, you have believed in vain."

Believing in Jesus and His every word is so essential to being a Christian. Why? John sheds more light on believing. Read John 14:1–4. Let's keep our Bibles in front of us while we go back over a few segments of what Jesus was saying and getting across to the disciples.

Here's a little background before we start: In John chapters 12 and 13 Jesus is talking about His betrayal and His death.

This talk just made the disciples confused and distraught. In John chapter 14, Jesus encourages them and gives them hope for now and the future.

John 14:1–4 paraphrased: Jesus said, "You believe in God, you can also believe in Me. We will not leave you hanging out there on your own. We have a plan for you now and in the future. So take heart in what I tell you. You cannot come with Me at this time because We have work for you to do. Later on you will be able to come and live with Us. We will have a place for you with Us. I am telling you this very truth now so that you will know and believe Me when I say that I am going to prepare the place for you, and when the time is right I will return and take you there. You should know the way to that place."

These words of Jesus now set up the big question from Thomas found in John 14:5–7, paraphrasing: Jesus said, "Okay Thomas, one more time—I am the way and the truth and the life. There is absolutely no other way to the Father. None. Period. To know Me is to know the Father. You need to know and understand this fact. Seeing Me and knowing Me is to know the Father."

After Jesus said these things, it sets up the big question from Philip. He must have been asleep! Paraphrasing John 14:8–11, "Philip, you men have been with Me for over three years now and you still don't know who I am? I have been teaching you about Myself, especially through the miracles I have performed, showing My true self to you all of these years—and you come up with the request for Me to show you the Father? You must be kidding!

Paraphrasing John 14:12–14, Jesus said, "Listen up! The truth is that you must believe in Me and My Father. You who believe will continue the work I have been doing here on earth. Not only continuing My work, but you will even do greater work than I have done. Here are some reasons why you will be able to do great works. One, as I am working in you and through you, the Father will be glorified. Two, believers will be able to ask the Father anything in My name and He will give it to them. And three, if you ask anything in My name, I will give it to you."

John 14 is one chapter to which we should anchor ourselves. We will see this more clearly as we continue to study the rest of John 14 in the next two chapters of this book. Let me briefly explain a little about the first three chapters in this book:

Chapter 1—Believe
Chapter 2—Love
Chapter 3—Obey

These three are intermingled with each other. One has to believe in order to love and then one can obey.

Now back to *believe*. The purpose of John's gospel is found in John 20:31 "But these are written that you may believe that Jesus is the Messiah, the Son of God, and that by believing you may have life in his name."

9. What was Paul's warning in 1 Corinthians 15:2?

10. What does Jesus promise believers in John 14:1–4?

11. What is the only way to the Father in John 14:5–7?

12. Who does Jesus say He is in John 14:8–11?

13. What is the believer's work in John 14:12–14?

14. How do believers accomplish this work?

15. In the three portions of scripture revealing God's plan for salvation, circle each person of the Trinity.

State our motto concerning God's Word.

Recite the memory verse for this chapter and also from Getting Started.

Note: In preparation for chapter 2,
you will need a dictionary

Chapter 2

The Loving Christian

Memory Verse: Mark 12:30–31
> Love the Lord your God with all your heart and with all your soul and with all your mind and with all your strength.' The second is this: 'Love your neighbor as yourself.' There is no commandment greater than these.

We are going to start this chapter by doing a little project. It is necessary for you to read all of 1 Corinthians 13. Then go back to 1 Corinthians 13:4–8 and you will find the definition of what love is and what love is not. You will need a dictionary to define the words written below in order to understand the deeper meaning of these words.

What love is: What love is not:

Patient   Envy

Kind   Boast

Review Chapter 2
The Loving Christian

1. What is the Biblical definition of love?

2. Does God's Word allow any "wiggle room" in the way we love Him?

3. In John 13:34–35, as believers, is loving each other an option or a command?

4. In 1 John 4:16, what is the evidence that we are living in God?

5. In 2 John 6, how does a believer show love for God?

6. In Colossians 3:12–14 list the virtues God's people must have in their lives?

7. What is the one thing these virtues can bring?

8. From the three negative love references Luke 16:13, Luke 12:34 and 1 John 2:15, what two things keep us from loving God?

9. In John 14, what does Jesus promise to those who love Him?

10. In John 14, what are the two things we do that bring the Father's and the Son's love to us?

11. According to John 14:15–16, if we love and obey Jesus, what will that bring us?

State our motto concerning God's Word.

Recite the memory verses.

ask God to help us do His will. This will bring glory to the Father and also show that we belong to Him.

Verse 9: Very simple: Remain in His love.

Verse 10: Jesus gives a tip on how to remain in His love. Keep Jesus' commands and you will continue in His love.

Verse 11: Here is another reward for remaining in Him: Complete joy for we who have His joy in us. Wow!

We are finally out of the vineyard. We could ask, "What does all of that have to do with this chapter on obedience?" Well, Jesus is speaking and we are to keep His word as well as any specific command. This is a great lesson on obedience.

If you have any doubts or questions about the interpretation of the illustration of the vine and branches, read John chapters 14, 15 and 16, keeping the illustration in the context of what Jesus was teaching His disciples at this time. Ask God to show you. Scripture will always interpret itself.

1 John 5:3-4a

> In fact, this is love for God: to keep his commands. And his commands are not burdensome, for everyone born of God overcomes the world.

Evidence of our love for God is obeying His commands.

1 John 2:3

> We know that we have come to know Him if we keep His commands.

Very simply, if you want to know God, obey His commands!

As we read in 1 John 3:21–24, we have: Believe, love and obey—whom to believe, whom to love and whom to obey. This is the reason why the first three chapters in this study book are emphasized. Believing, loving and obeying are so interwoven. So we see that we cannot know God unless we are living a life of believing, loving and obeying Him. There are many more scriptures in the Bible that indicate this truth.

2 John 6
> And this is love: that we walk in obedience to his commands. As you have heard from the beginning, his command is that you walk in love.

Obedience is evidence that we love God and each other. Or is it the other way around? Again we cannot separate love and obey.

Read John 14:15–21.

Here is another combo of love and obey. We find in verses 16–20 there are rewards for loving and obeying. In verse 21 Jesus repeats what He said in verse 15.

Luke 11:28
> He replied, 'Blessed rather are those who hear the word of God and obey it.'

Again, we see more rewards for obeying God.

Acts 5:32
> We are witnesses of these things, and so is the Holy Spirit, whom God has given to those who obey him.

Read 1 John 5:1–5.

We are about to see more verses that include the three evidences of a real Christian; believing, loving and obeying. Believing is loving

9. What are two rewards for remaining in Christ?

10. How do we remain in Jesus' love?

11. What is the evidence that we know God in 1 John 2:3?

12. What does Jesus promise in John 14:16?

13. To whom does God give the Holy Spirit in Acts 5:32?

14. In Hebrews 5:9, who is it that receives eternal salvation?

15. According to the Great Commission, why do we make disciples?

State our motto for God's Word.

Recite all of the memory verses.

A Note To The Leader

Notice that Chapters 4 and 5 have a change of pace. Their purpose is to read a complete book of the Bible in a short time, realize what God is saying to each one and help to make it a joyful time. Relate to the class to read three chapters each day in Proverbs and answer the questions. If they do that daily they will finish the session on time.

Chapter 4

Wise Counsel For The Christian

Part 1

Memory Verse: Proverbs 9:10
> The fear of the Lord is the beginning of wisdom, and knowledge of the Holy One is understanding.

As we read the Book of Proverbs, let us keep in mind that we are seeking and finding wisdom and knowledge. Remember wisdom and knowledge are from God.

As we find each key word or phrase, we can jot them down and discuss the implications, good or bad, and see what the application is for us today. Even though this was written over three thousand years ago, there are abiding principles of God that are like Him. They, like Him, are for yesterday, today and forever.

In each chapter there are some things to notice as we study: The key words and phrases that will also bring about a theme for the chapter. Notice the overall theme of the Bible, which is the Sovereignty of God and the Responsibility of Man.

There are a few questions in each chapter to motivate your reading and thinking.

3. What is it the Lord detests and in what does He delight in verse 20?

4. What happens when we give generously and what happens when we withhold in verse 24?

Proverbs 12:
1. Who does the Lord condemn in verse 2?

2. Why won't a fool listen in verse 15?

3. In verse 22, what does the Lord detest and in what does He delight?

Proverbs 13:
1. What brings life and what brings ruin in verse 3?

2. What does pride bring in verse 10?

3. In your own words what do you think verse 12 means?

4. Why does it matter who your friends are in verse 20?

5. What is your opinion about this advice on childrearing in verse 24?

Proverbs 14:
There are a large amount of positive and negative verses that please God and don't please Him. We should take notice and do those things that please God.

In Chapter 14 list the things that please God.

Proverbs 15:
1. How do we handle wrath and anger in verse 1?

2. What displeases God and what pleases Him in verse 8?

3. In verse 33, what is the significance of wisdom, instruction and humility?

Proverbs 16:
1. What are man's ways and what are God's ways, and who is in charge in verses 1–4?

2. How does God deal with sin and evil in verse 6?

In 19:8–10, we see that wisdom nurtures a person's soul and builds good character.

In 19:23 we see that the satisfying life is a God-centered life.

Read Proverbs 20 and 21.
In 20:1, strong drink presumes to bring satisfaction but it really deceives.

In 20:4, what do lazy people accomplish?

In 20:19, beware of gossipers and don't associate with them.

What are two things that displease God in 20:23?

In 20:27, our spirit is the inner being that allows us to connect with God, and He uses it as light to express His truth.

In 21:1–2, we again see the sovereignty of God and the responsibility of man.

From what does choosing wise words keep you in 21:23?

How does the fool behave in 21:24?

What happens to the lazy one in 21:25?

Read Proverbs 22.

Teach a child the way of the Lord and what will be the result in 22:6, 15?

In Proverbs 22:17–24:22 list the thirty sayings of the wise.

In Proverbs 25, what is a wise man's rebuke like?

What is like reliance on the unfaithful in times of trouble?

What does verse 28 compare to a "city whose walls are broken through?"

In Proverbs 26, we find contrasts between the fool and the righteousness. Find these contrasts and underline a few verses that are meaningful to you in this chapter. Record them below and share your findings.

In Proverbs 27, find and list the qualities of the wise.

What makes a man happy is stewardship, not ownership.

List the blessings and character qualities of the righteous in Proverbs 28.

In Proverbs 29, find the contrasts between the wise and the fool then list them.

Pride brings a person down where humility exalts one, which is a universal law of God and seen throughout history.

Read Proverbs 30.

1. In verses 4 and 5, of whom are they speaking?

2. Why can we be satisfied with only our daily bread? (verses 8 and 9)

3. What are the four things that are never satisfied?

Proverbs 31:

List some of the virtues of the noble woman. Which one stands out the most to you?

As a Christian, our wisdom is Christ and comes from knowing Christ.

Colossians 2:2–3

> My goal is that they may be encouraged in heart and united in love, so that they may have the full riches of complete understanding, in order that they may know the mystery of God, namely, Christ, in whom are hidden all the treasures of wisdom and knowledge.

What is our motto concerning God's Word?

Recite all 7 of the memory verses.

Chapter 6

The Christian In Relation To The Church

Memory Verse: Matthew 16:18
> And I tell you that you are Peter, and on this rock I will build my church, and the gates of Hades will not overcome it.

Read Matthew 16:13–18.

There are some who believe Christ was saying that He would build His Church on Peter. There are two rocks involved in this passage. One is Peter, the small rock, and the other one is Jesus, the foundation rock.

Peter, *petros*: "Peter, this has the designative meaning "rock" or "individual stone."

Rock, *petra*: "rock, bedrock, rocky crag, or other large rock formation, in contrast to individual stones, with a focus that is a suitable, solid foundation: - rock."

In this passage Jesus referred to Peter saying, "Simon, son of Jonah . . . you are *Peter* (individual stone)." Peter's reply to Jesus was, "You are the Messiah, the Son of the living God." And Jesus says, "And on this *petra* (solid foundation), I will build my church."

This is the purpose of the church:

2 Corinthians 5:18–20,

> All this is from God, who reconciled us to himself through Christ and gave us the ministry of reconciliation: that God was reconciling the world to himself in Christ, not counting people's sins against them. And he has committed to us the message of reconciliation.
>
> We are therefore Christ's ambassadors, as though God were making his appeal through us. We implore you on Christ's behalf: Be reconciled to God.

We have work to do! Let's do it!

Review Chapter 6
The Christian In Relation To The Church

1. In Matthew 16:18, do you think Jesus is going to build His church on Peter? Explain.

2. What is the foundation of the church according to Peter in 1 Peter 2:4–8, and Paul in 1 Corinthians 3:11?

3. List some of the terms and objects that are used to describe the church but are not the church?

4. What is your definition of the church?

5. From 1 Corinthians 12:1–6, list the work of each one of the Trinity in these verses.

6. Beginning in 1 Corinthians 12:12, does Paul place any part more highly regarded than another? Explain.

Let's continue with the heart in the following scriptures:

Romans 10:9–10

> If you declare with your mouth, "Jesus is Lord," and believe in your heart that God raised him from the dead, you will be saved. For it is with your heart that you believe and are justified, and it is with your mouth that you profess your faith and are saved."

In the above scripture, what parts are involved in salvation?

Colossians 3:23–24a

> Whatever you do, work at it with all your heart, as working for the Lord, not for human masters, since you know that you will receive an inheritance from the Lord as a reward.

Ephesians 1:18–19a

> I pray also that the eyes of your heart may be enlightened in order that you may know the hope to which he has called you, the riches of his glorious inheritance in his holy people, and his incomparably great power for us who believe.

In these verses, what does Paul pray that our hearts will grasp?

Soul:

We will take the following reference in Psalms and comment again. As we read these Psalms let's do a little soul searching.

Read Psalm 62:1–2 and Psalm 42:1–2a. What do you think the comparison is in these references?

In Psalm 63:1, how is this verse connected to Psalm 42:1–2a?

Read Matthew 11:28–29. Describe what you think a troubled soul is like and what is the rest Jesus gives to our souls?

In reading 1 Peter 1:8–9, what does Peter say is the end result of our faith in Christ?

Spirit:
Read Matthew 26:40–41. In this case, we can see how important it is to watch and pray for the spirit to overcome the weakness of the body.

Luke 1:46–47, when Mary said, "My soul glorifies the Lord and my spirit rejoices in God my Savior", it appears Mary was responding with her *inner* self and her *spirit* that communicates with God.

John 3:5–8

> Jesus answered, "Very truly I tell you, no one can enter the kingdom of God unless they are born of water and the Spirit. Flesh gives birth to flesh, but the Spirit gives birth to spirit. You should not be surprised at my saying, 'You must be born again.' The wind blows wherever it pleases. You hear its sound, but you cannot tell where it comes from or where it is going. So it is with everyone born of the Spirit.

This is a truth that God's Spirit connects with our spirit. Being born again can only happen in a spiritual sense. Continue with this thought and read Romans 8:16. This is an indication again that we are born into God's family.

Read John 4:23–24, where Jesus explains the only way to be in contact with God is through the spirit within us – ours and His.

Romans 8:10

> But if Christ is in you, then even though your body is subject to death because of sin, the spirit gives life because of righteousness.

What is the key to having a "body dead because of sin" and a "spirit alive because of righteousness?"

1 Corinthians 6:17

> But whoever is united with the Lord is one with him in spirit.

The definition of *unite* is: "Unite–*kollao*–to join, associate with, cling to; to be united, stuck to, piled up; to stay near, follow".

This simply means our spirit bears witness to His Spirit. We are one.

Review Chapter 7
God Wants The Whole Christian, Part 1

1. According to Psalm 51:10, what is the solution for a deceitful heart?

2. According to Psalm 15:1–2, what was David's question and answer?

3. According to 2 Timothy 3:16–17, is the Old Testament as relevant today as it was before Christ?

4. In Colossians 3:23–24, our work attitude should be what?

5. In 1 Peter 1:8–9, what does Peter say is the end result of our faith in Jesus Christ?

6. In John 3:1–8, in what is the Spirit involved?

spiritual relationship with Him and also, eventually, if we offer our bodies to sin, it will destroy us.

Romans 12:1-2, have a bearing on all of Romans 6. It is key for knowing God's will for our whole life.

Read Romans 12:1-2.

This is another winning combination of giving our bodies and minds to God. In Romans 12:1 Paul says, "Therefore, I urge you."

"Urge, *parakaleo*, to ask, beg, plead; to comfort, encourage, exhort, to call, invite."

"... in view of God's mercy, to offer your bodies as a living sacrifice, holy and pleasing to God – this is your true and proper worship ..." (Romans 12:1)

When we consider and understand God's mercy and what He has given us in and through Christ, step one is offering ourselves to God, which should be a natural response to Him.

Paul talks about holiness in Romans 6:19.

In Romans 12:2, step two is the winning combination: "Do not conform to the pattern of this world, but be transformed by the renewing of your mind."

A Christian who is conforming to the pattern of this world, needs to have his brain washed (be transformed by the renewing and washing of his mind) for and by God through putting God's Word in his heart. "Be transformed by the renewing of your mind.", because we know the god of this world system is Satan, and his pattern for our lives is a counterfeit of God's pattern.

Are you wondering what God's will is for your life? If you are, follow step one, offer yourself to God, and step two, offer your mind to God. Then you will know God's will for your life.

The result of offering our bodies to God and renewing our minds is knowing God's will for our lives: "Then you will be able to test and approve what God's will is – his good, pleasing and perfect will." (Romans 12:2b)

Mind:
Isaiah 26:3
> You will keep in perfect peace those whose minds are steadfast, because they trust in you.

Ask yourself where your mind is focused. As children of God we must focus our minds on Him. Here are some verses that will help us.

Again, read Romans 12:2. We just commented on the critical truth of Romans 12:2 in the last segment. It is crucial to emphasize the importance of the Spirit-controlled mind.

Romans 8:6
> The mind governed by the flesh is death, but the mind governed by the Spirit is life and peace.

Read 2 Corinthians 10:5, Colossians 3:2, Ephesians 4:22–24, and Philippians 2:1–2.

In Romans 8:29, what is God's ultimate plan for those He adopts?

Don't we wish it would all be automatic? In reading the Bible there is nothing that happens without cause and effect. The good or bad we cause, we will reap the effect.

ARMOR OF GOD

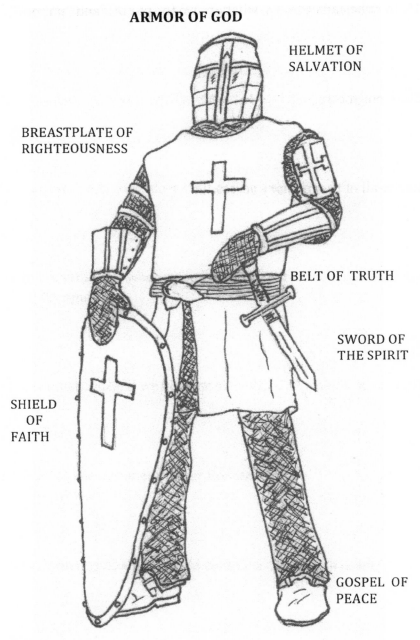

Sketch by Sandra Johnson

The Weapons Of Battle For The Christian, Illustrated

Read Ephesians 6:10–18. Notice the illustration of the armor of God and how each piece fits.

In the next eight chapters, we are going to learn how to do battle with the enemy. We need to have our minds focused on defensive and offensive weapons of war.

On the opposite page, we have a man in ancient armor, wearing the typical battlefield attire. For all practical purposes, we need to look at and see the similarities of modern day warfare compared to the ancient day warfare.

There are offensive weapons, defensive weapons, battlefield strategies, knowing your enemy and how to survive. In preparation for battle there always needs to be basic training. Basic training includes physical training, mental training and operational training, i.e., knowing the weapons, use of the weapons, and survival tactics on how to protect ourselves from whatever and however the enemy is trying to defeat us.

Modern day tactics have armor, i.e., tanks, troop carriers, other vehicles, bulletproof vests, steel helmets, combat boots and combat dress. The penetrating weapons are the ammunition. The comparison is not realistic in the sense that modern warfare weapons are for physical battle fields, and the weapons Paul talks about, the use of God's full armor, is for spiritual battle fields.

Even though, in our country, we have the world's mightiest military force, it cannot have any effect on the spiritual battles we believers go through.

The real comparison is that we can be killed or wounded in either battlefield. God has given us these weapons so that we can stand firm, defeat the enemy and win the battle. Wouldn't it make sense that we believers have basic training in spiritual warfare, and know and understand how to use these weapons in order to have the victory?

John 14:6

>Jesus answered, 'I am the way and the truth and the life. No one comes to the Father except through me'.

John 16:13

>But when he, the Spirit of truth, comes, he will guide you into all the truth. He will not speak on his own; he will speak only what He hears, and He will tell you what is yet to come.

According to these scriptures, and others, Jesus and the Holy Spirit are truth, *absolute truth*. As for us who believe, we can know and have the absolute truth in us. This truth is what makes up the belt of truth the apostle Paul exhorts us put on, so that we may be able to stand firm.

Here are various scriptures that declare what truth is and does:

John 1:14

>The Word became flesh and made his dwelling among us. We have seen his glory, the glory of the one and only Son, who came from the Father, full of grace and truth.

John 3:21

>But whoever lives by the truth comes into the light, so that it may be seen plainly that what they have done has been done in the sight of God.

2 Peter 1:12

>So I will always remind you of these things, even though you know them and are firmly established in the truth you now have.

Ephesians 1:13

>And you also were included in Christ when you heard the message of truth, the gospel of your salvation. When you

believed, you were marked in him with a seal, the promised Holy Spirit.

John 17:17

Sanctify them by the truth; your word is truth.

2 John 1–3

The elder,
To the lady chosen by God and to her children, whom I love in the truth – and not I only, but also all who know the truth – because of the truth, which lives in us and will be with us forever:
Grace, mercy and peace from God the Father and from Jesus Christ, the Father's Son, will be with us in truth and love.

Now we will do some reading and discussing of truths that Jesus wants us to understand. Following are various scriptures where Jesus makes the statement, "I tell you the truth." Read and write down what truth Jesus wants us to understand in:

Matthew 5:18

Matthew 5:25–26

Matthew 6:2

Matthew 6:5

Matthew 6:16

Matthew 8:5–10

Matthew 10:11–15

Matthew 10:16–23

Matthew 10:42

Matthew 11:11

Matthew 13:16–17

Matthew 17:20

Matthew 18:3

Matthew 18:12–14

Matthew 18:15–20

Matthew 19:21–24

Matthew 19:28–30

Matthew 21:18–22

Matthew 25:1–13

Matthew 25:31–46

Matthew 26:6–13

Mark 12:41–44

John 3

John 5:16–30

John 6:25–59

John 8:31–47

John 8:58

John 10:1–21

John 13:16

John 13:20

John 14:11–14

John 16:7

The apostle Paul tells us to take our stand with the belt of truth buckled around our waist.

Belt: "*osphys* – waist, loins, body; belt – dressed ready for service; prepare for action."

As we can see, this definition means more than just a sash. It means all of the above. Truth should be in our lives as we are dressed for service and prepared for action. This is how we take our stand. We must know the truth and know how to apply it because Satan is the father of lies, and he will twist and turn and counterfeit everything in order to side-line, wound or kill God's people. "The truth will set you free."

Review Chapter 9
The Belt Of Truth

1. Can we believe that there is absolute truth?

2. Where can we find it?

3. What is the source of absolute truth?

4. If there is no absolute truth, what will take its place?

5. According to John 8:31–47, from what does the truth set us free?

6. As a defensive weapon, how does the truth affect your stand?

7. As a Christian, what does the truth mean to you?

What is our motto concerning God's word?

Recite all of the memory verses

Note: The next chapters have a lot of scripture in them. I encourage you to get a notepad or a journal, read each of the scriptures and jot down what the Holy Spirit tells you, what jumps out at you, what touches you, what impacts you. Have fun and be blessed!

Chapter 10

The Breastplate Of Righteousness

Memory Verse: Matthew 6:33
> But seek first his kingdom and his righteousness, and all these things will be given to you as well.

Breastplate: "*thorax* – breastplate."

Righteousness: "*dikaiosyne* – what is right, justice, the act of doing what is in agreement with God's standards, the state of being in proper relationship with God."

As we study this chapter keep in mind that our righteousness is Jesus Christ.

Matthew 5:6
> Blessed are those who hunger and thirst for righteousness, for they will be filled.

Romans 1:17
> For in the gospel the righteousness of God is revealed - a righteousness that is by faith from first to last, just as it is written: 'The righteous will live by faith.'

7. In Romans 6:15–23, if we are not slaves to righteousness, then to what are we slaves?

8. If Christ is living in us, what are the results in Romans 8:9–11?

9. What is the kingdom of God like according to Romans 14:17–18?

10. What does God ask us to "take off" and "put on" in Ephesians 4:22–24?

11. From what does God ask us to flee in 2 Timothy 2:22?

12. Where is the home of righteousness in 2 Peter 3:13?

What is our motto according to God's word?

State all of the memory verses.

Chapter 11

Feet Fitted With The Gospel Of Peace

Memory Verse: Romans 1:16

> For I am not ashamed of the gospel, because it is the power of God that brings salvation to everyone who believes: first to the Jew, then to the Gentile.

Gospel: "*euangelizo*, v. – to preach the good news"

Gospel: "*euangelion*, n. – the good news"

1 Corinthians 15:1–5

> Now, brothers and sisters, I want to remind you of the gospel I preached to you, which you received and on which you have taken your stand. By this gospel you are saved, if you hold firmly to the word I preached to you. Otherwise, you have believed in vain.
>
> For what I received I passed on to you as of first importance: that Christ died for our sins according to the Scriptures, that he was buried, that he was raised on the third day according to the Scriptures, and that he appeared to Cephas, and then to the Twelve.

Chapter 12

The Shield Of Faith

Memory Verse: Romans 5:1-2

> Therefore, since we have been justified through faith, we
> have peace with God through our Lord Jesus Christ, through
> whom we have gained access by faith into this grace in
> which we now stand. And we boast in the hope of the glory
> of God.

Faith: "*pistis* – faith, faithfulness, belief, trust, with an implication
that actions based on that trust may follow: "the faith" often refers
to the Christian system of belief and lifestyle."

Hebrews 11 has been referred to as the "Hall of Faith" chapter in
the Bible. As we read Hebrews 11, remember we are considering the
shield of faith that is part of God's armor, a protective weapon. We
will find out what faith is, why one must have faith and how faith
is played out in all of the faithful names mentioned.

List the persons and their acts of faith below in verses 1–40.

<u>NAME</u>   <u>ACTS OF FAITH</u>

Ephesians 3:16–17a

> I pray that out of his glorious riches he may strengthen you with power through his Spirit in your inner being, so that Christ may dwell in your hearts through faith.

Philippians 3:9

> and be found in him, not having a righteousness of my own that comes from the law, but that which is through faith in Christ – the righteousness that comes from God on the basis of faith.

1 John 5:4–5

> for everyone born of God overcomes the world. This is the victory that has overcome the world, even our faith. Who is it that overcomes the world? Only the one who believes that Jesus is the Son of God.

List what we have in Christ and how this is possible in 1 Peter 1:3–5.

2 Corinthians 5:7

> For we live by faith, not by sight.

1 Peter 1:8–9

> Though you have not seen him, you love him; and even though you do not see him now, you believe in him and are filled with an inexpressible and glorious joy, for you are receiving the end result of your faith, the salvation of your souls.

Colossians 2:6–7

> So then, just as you received Christ Jesus as Lord, continue to live your lives in him, rooted and built up in

him, strengthened in the faith as you were taught, and overflowing with thankfulness.

1 Peter 5:8–9

Be alert and of sober mind. Your enemy the devil prowls around like a roaring lion looking for someone to devour. Resist him, standing firm in the faith, because you know that the family of believers throughout the world is undergoing the same kind of sufferings.

If our faith protects us from Satan's attempt to penetrate our lives, wouldn't it be to our advantage to have the biggest shield that we could carry? Scripture tells us, faith comes by hearing and that we can be strengthened by our faith by being taught the Word of God. The more Word, the more faith, the bigger the shield.

Review Chapter 12
The Shield Of Faith

1. What does 1 John 5:4–5 say is our victory over the world?

2. After reading Hebrews 11, do the lives of the people mentioned define faith? (see Hebrews 11:1,6) Discuss.

3. According to Romans 10:17, from where does faith come?

4. According to Philippians 3:9, how are we credited with righteousness?

5. In Ephesians 3:16–17, how does Christ dwell in our hearts?

6. What is the goal of our faith in 1 Peter 1:8–9?

7. How do we resist the devil in 1 Peter 5:8–9?

8. In Colossians 2:6–7, can your faith be strengthened? How? What is the result?

What is our motto according to God's Word?

Recite all of the memory verses.

Acts 4:10–12

Acts 13:26

Acts 13:47

Romans 1:16

> For I am not ashamed of the gospel, because it is the power of God that brings salvation to everyone who believes: first to the Jew, then to the Gentile.

Romans 13:11

> And do this, understanding the present time: The hour has come for you to wake up from your slumber, because our salvation is nearer now than when we first believed.

2 Corinthians 6:2

> For he says, 'In the time of my favor I heard you, and in the day of salvation I helped you.'
>
> I tell you, now is the time of God's favor, now is the day of salvation." (see Isaiah 49:8)

Is there an urgency within these words and how urgent is it?

2 Corinthians 7:10

> Godly sorrow brings repentance that leads to salvation and leaves no regret, but worldly sorrow brings death.

Ephesians 1:13a

> And you also were included in Christ when you heard the message of truth, the gospel of your salvation.

Philippians 2:12–13

> Therefore, my dear friends, as you have always obeyed - not only in my presence, but now much more in my absence – continue to work out your salvation with fear and trembling, for it is God who works in you to will and to act in order to fulfill his good purpose.

What do you think this verse means?

Work out: "*katergazomai* – to produce, accomplish, bring about, achieving, carry out, committed, develops."

This is another example of God's sovereignty and the responsibility of man.

2 Timothy 2:10

> Therefore I endure everything for the sake of the elect, that they too may obtain the salvation that is in Christ Jesus, with eternal glory.

Hebrews 1:14

> Are not all angels ministering spirits sent to serve those who will inherit salvation?

Hebrews 2:3–4

> How shall we escape if we ignore so great a salvation? This salvation, which was first announced by the Lord, was confirmed to us by those who heard him. God also testified to it by signs, wonders and various miracles, and by gifts of the Holy Spirit distributed according to his will.

Here is a note about the Sword of the Spirit and why it is studied in two parts in this book.

Part 1 is all about the Spirit because we need to know who He is and what He does.

Part 2 is about the Sword, which is the Word of God.

We will find throughout our study and any further study of the New Testament that the Holy Spirit does not work outside the boundary of the Word of God. We must remember that the Holy Spirit is not wielding the Sword. In this case it is we who take up the Sword because the Holy Spirit is living within us.

Chapter 14

The Sword Of The Spirit

Part 1

<u>The Spirit</u>

Memory Verse: John 14:15–17a
> If you love me, keep my commands. And I will ask the Father, and he will give you another Advocate to help you and be with you forever – the Spirit of truth.

Sword: "*machaira* – sword or edge sword; *stoma* – mouth; by extension: edge (of a sword): mouth, mouths, lips, face, testimony, words, began to speak, edge sword, might say, speak, spoken freely, sword."

Spirit: "*pneuma* – wind, breath, things which are commonly perceived as having no material substance; . . . God the Holy Spirit."

Advocate: "*parakletos* – an advocate, comforter, helper, one who encourages and comforts; in the New Testament it refers exclusively to the Holy Spirit and Jesus Christ; one who speaks in defense."

Here are some key verses about the promised Holy Spirit.

Review Chapter 14
The Sword Of The Spirit, Part 1

1. In the Gospel of John, what chapter and verse first tell of the promised Holy Spirit?

2. What is the Holy Spirit's purpose when He comes to a believer in John 16:13–15?

3. In Acts 1:8, what happens when the believer receives the Holy Spirit?

4. According to Paul in 1 Corinthians 2:9–14, how do we understand God's revelation to us?

5. According to 1 Corinthians 6:19–20, why should we honor God with our bodies?

6. In 2 Corinthians 3:6, what is the difference between the old and new covenants?

7. Why is there "now no condemnation" according to Romans 8:2?

8. In Romans 8:9–10, how can you not live by the sinful nature? What do these words say if you do not have the Spirit of Christ in you?

9. In Romans 8:12–14, what is our obligation?

10. What is the Kingdom of God according to Romans 14:17–18?

11. In Ephesians 1:17, why should we ask for wisdom and revelation?

12. In 1 John 3:24, how do we know that we live in Jesus? Hint: there are two.

What is our motto?

Recite the memory verses.

John S. Johnson

In Ephesians 1:13–14, when is one included in salvation?

In 1 Thessalonians 2:13, how did the people receive Paul's preaching?

2 Timothy 2:15 indicates that a person who does not handle the Word of God correctly will be ashamed.

What is Paul's claim in Titus 1:1–3?

According to Hebrews 1:3, what does the Word do?

In James 1:18–25, what does the Word do for us?

In James 1:19–21, what are we not to do and what are we to do?

In James 1:22–25, what are we to do about the Word of God?

According to Peter in 1 Peter 1:23–25, how is one born again?

What does John call Jesus in 1 John 1:1?

What six names are given to Jesus in Revelation 19:11–16?

The Sword, which is the Word, is our only offensive weapon. Knowing God's Word and allowing the Spirit to speak it through us will defeat the enemy and save our lives. This is why we should memorize God's Word.

What is our motto?

Recite all of your memory verses.

Time for prayer:
    1 Corinthians 7:5

Prayer for children:
    Matthew 19:13

Prayer for faith:
    Philemon 6

Prayer for everything:
    1 Timothy 4:4–5
    Philippians 4:6–7

Prayer for health and well being:
    3 John 2

Prayer for enemies:
    Luke 6:27–28

Prayer for farewell:
    Acts 21:5–6

Prayer for God's will:
    Romans 8:26–27
    Jude 20

Notice in the two scriptures above, when it says to pray in the Spirit, it stresses that the prayer should be requesting God's will.

How not to pray:
    Matthew 6:5–6

In the above verses what is wrong with these prayers?

This chapter does not exhaust all the different prayers and ways to pray in the Bible. If you would like to do a good personal drill on prayer, read the Book of Psalms and list all the prayers and for what was prayed.

- Image of Christ: A disciple's goal is to become more like Jesus. This is also God's goal for us—Chapter 8 (Romans 8:29)

One cannot pretend or perform these characteristics, and they are not acquired by works or by any worldly teaching. They can only be gained by living in Christ, and He in us. This is who we are in Christ.

CONGRATULATIONS!

You have finished
What Makes a Christian a Disciple of Christ

If you're still not sure what makes a Christian a disciple of Christ, keep studying God's Word; *He will tell you!*

It is my prayer that you have gained more knowledge of Jesus Christ and you will continue to grow up in Him to the glory of God.

Commit to have your own personal daily devotions and prayer time with God and devotions with your family. Get involved in Bible studies and small groups, attend church regularly, share your faith and allow God to guide and direct what He has for you in His perfect will.

Made in the USA
Monee, IL
25 May 2021